cute critter pu
to crochet

Crochet doesn't get cuter than this! Six adorable animals make themselves useful as children's purse pets. Bright button eyes and lots of individual detail give the "critters" their appealing personalities. A flap closure keeps necessities safely inside the handbag. Crochet a puppy, kitten, bunny, bear, piggy, or cow. Your little sweetheart will be delighted to take her new animal friend with her everywhere she goes.

There's just something special about a great purse. If you're like me, you have an entire collection of purses and bags to match changing moods and toting capacities. Most women, from girlie girls to "grown-ups" like me, understand the power of the purse…attitude, confidence, and the certainty that you've got it all together…so many good things in one complete package. I can think of at least one young lady who'd love to have a cuddly critter purse (and so would I, for that matter, but then I'd be forced to seriously downsize from my current twenty-pound carryall!). Whether you're young or just young at heart, go ahead and add a great new purse to your collection. Then send me a photo at KnitCrochetEditor@leisurearts.com so I can envy your crocheted creation!

Cheryl

Cheryl Johnson
Knit & Crochet Publication Director

LEISURE ARTS, INC.
Little Rock, AR

basic purse

■■■□ INTERMEDIATE

FINISHED SIZE: 11" long x 6" tall (28 cm x 15 cm) (excluding Handles)

MATERIALS

Medium Weight Yarn
   [7 ounces, 364 yards
   (198 grams, 333 meters) per skein]:
   Bear
      Black - 1 skein
      Brown - 1 skein
   Bunny
      White - 1 skein
      Pink - small amount
   Cow
      White - 1 skein
      Black - 1 skein
      Pink - small amount
      Brown - small amount
   Kitten
      Grey - 1 skein
      Pink - small amount
      Black - small amount
   Piggy
      Pink - 1 skein
      Black - small amount
   Puppy
      Brown - 1 skein
      Black - 1 skein
Crochet hook, size J (6 mm) **or** size needed for gauge
Polyester fiberfill stuffing
5/8" (16 mm) Black rounded shank buttons - 2 for each Purse (for eyes)
One button - no larger than 1/2" (12 mm)
Sewing needle and thread
Yarn needle
3/4" (2 cm) Pom-pom - 1 each (for Kitten and Bunny) and craft glue
Ribbon - 1 yard (1 meter)

GAUGE: 13 sc and 14 rnds/rows = 4" (10 cm)

Gauge Swatch: 4" (10 cm) square
Ch 14.
Row 1: Sc in second ch from hook and in each ch across: 13 sc.
Rows 2-14: Ch 1, turn; sc in each sc across. Finish off.

STITCH GUIDE

DECREASE
Pull up a loop in next 2 sc, YO and draw through all 3 loops on hook **(counts as one sc)**.

Note: Loop a short piece of yarn around any stitch to mark Rnd 1 as **right** side **(now and throughout)**.

BODY
BASE
With color specified in individual instructions, ch 13.

Rnd 1 (Right side)**:** 2 Sc in second ch from hook, sc in each ch across to last ch, 3 sc in last ch; working in free loops of beginning ch **(Fig. 3b, page 22)**; sc in next 10 chs and in same st as first sc; do **not** join, place marker to mark beginning of rnd **(see Markers, page 21)**: 26 sc.

Rnd 2: 2 Sc in each of next 2 sc, sc in next 10 sc, 2 sc in each of next 3 sc, sc in next 10 sc, 2 sc in next sc: 32 sc.

Rnd 3: 2 Sc in next sc, sc in next sc, 2 sc in next sc, sc in next 11 sc, 2 sc in next sc, (sc in next sc, 2 sc in next sc) twice, sc in next 11 sc, 2 sc in next sc, sc in next sc; slip st in Back Loop Only of next sc **(Fig. 2, page 22)**: 38 sc.

Rnd 4: Ch 1, working in Back Loops Only, 2 sc in same st, (sc in next sc, 2 sc in next sc) twice, sc in next 12 sc, 2 sc in next sc, (sc in next sc, 2 sc in next sc) 3 times, sc in next 12 sc, 2 sc in next sc, sc in next sc; join with slip st to **both** loops of first sc, finish off: 46 sc.

PURSE

Work same as Base through Rnd 4; do **not** finish off.

Rnd 5 (Joining rnd)**:** With **wrong** sides of Base and Body together, matching stitches; working through **both** loops of **both** pieces; ch 1, sc in each sc around; do **not** join, place marker to mark beginning of rnd: 46 sc.

Rnds 6-27: Sc in each sc around.

Rnd 28: Sc in each sc around; slip st in next sc, finish off leaving a long end for sewing.

Turn Body **wrong** side out with Rnds 1-16 forming inner Purse, then fold Body at Rnd 17 to form outer Purse so Rnd 28 is at edge of Purse Base. Stuff evenly between inner and outer Purse.

Working through free loops of sc on Rnd 3 of Base and both loops of sc of Rnd 28 on Purse easing to fit, whipstitch bottom of Purse **(Fig. 5, page 22)**.

HEAD

With color specified in individual instructions, ch 3; join with slip st to form a ring.

Rnd 1 (Right side)**:** 2 Sc in each ch around; do **not** join, place marker to mark beginning of rnd: 6 sc.

Rnd 2: 2 Sc in each sc around: 12 sc.

Rnd 3: (Sc in next sc, 2 sc in next sc) around: 18 sc.

Rnd 4: (Sc in next 2 sc, 2 sc in next sc) around: 24 sc.

Rnd 5: (Sc in next 3 sc, 2 sc in next sc) around: 30 sc.

Rnd 6: (Sc in next 4 sc, 2 sc in next sc) around: 36 sc.

Rnd 7: (Sc in next 5 sc, 2 sc in next sc) around: 42 sc.

Rnd 8: (Sc in next 6 sc, 2 sc in next sc) around: 48 sc.

Rnds 9 and 10: Sc in each sc around.

Rnd 11: (Sc in next 2 sc, decrease) around: 36 sc.

Rnd 12: (Sc in next sc, decrease) around: 24 sc.

Rnd 13: Decrease around; slip st in next sc, finish off leaving a long end for sewing: 12 sc.

Stuff Head.

PAW (Make 4)

With color specified in individual instructions, ch 3; join with slip st to form a ring.

Rnd 1 (Right side)**:** Ch 1, 2 sc in each ch around; do **not** join, place marker to mark beginning of rnd: 6 sc.

Rnds 2 and 3: 2 Sc in each sc around: 24 sc.

Rnd 4: Sc in each sc around.

Rnd 5: Decrease 6 times, sc in next 12 sc: 18 sc.

Instructions continued on page 4.

Rnd 6: (Sc in next 4 sc, decrease) around: 15 sc.

Rnds 7-9: Sc in each sc around.

Rnd 10: Sc in each sc around; slip st in next sc, finish off leaving a long end for sewing.

Stuff Paw.

LEG (Make 4)
With Black, ch 3; join with slip st to form a ring.

Rnd 1 (Right side): Ch 1, 2 sc in each ch around; do **not** join, place marker to mark beginning of rnd: 6 sc.

Rnd 2: 2 Sc in each sc around: 12 sc.

Rnd 3: (Sc in next 3 sc, 2 sc in next sc) around; slip st in next sc; cut Black: 15 sc.

Rnd 4: With **right** side facing, join color specified in individual instructions with sc in same st as slip st **(see Joining With Sc, page 22)**; sc in each sc around.

Rnds 5-10: Sc in each sc around.

Rnd 11: Sc in each sc around; slip st in next sc, finish off leaving a long end for sewing.

Stuff Leg.

HANDLE (Make 2)
Stuff Handles as you work.

With color specified in individual instructions, ch 6; join with slip st to form a ring.

Rnd 1 (Right side): Sc in each ch around; do **not** join, place marker to mark beginning of rnd: 6 sc.

Rnds 2-50: Sc in each sc around.

Rnd 51: Sc in each sc around; slip st in next sc, finish off leaving a long end for sewing.

FLAP
With color specified in individual instructions, ch 3; join with slip st to form a ring.

Rnd 1 (Right side): 2 Sc in each ch around; do **not** join, place marker to mark beginning of rnd: 6 sc.

Rnd 2: 2 Sc in each sc around: 12 sc.

Rnd 3: Sc in next 2 sc, ch 2, skip next 2 sc **(buttonhole made)**, sc in next 4 sc, ch 2, skip next 2 sc **(buttonhole made)**, sc in next 2 sc: 8 sc and 2 ch-2 sps.

Rnd 4: Working in each sc and in each ch, (sc in next 3 sts, 2 sc in next st) around: 15 sc.

Rnd 5: (Sc in next 4 sc, 2 sc in next sc) around: 18 sc.

Rnd 6: (Sc in next 2 sc, 2 sc in next sc) around: 24 sc.

Rnd 7: (Sc in next 3 sc, 2 sc in next sc) around: 30 sc.

Rnds 8-16: Sc in each sc around: 30 sc.

Rnd 17: Sc in each sc around; slip st in next sc, finish off leaving a long end for sewing.

FINISHING
For children younger than three years of age, replace all buttons with embroidery or felt.

Using photo as a guide for placement:
Sew Head to Body.
Sew Handles to Rnd 17 of Body with one end of each Handle on either side of Head and remaining ends on Rnd 17 opposite Head and leaving room for Tail.
Sew Paws or Legs to Base.
Flatten Rnd 17 of Flap, lining buttonholes up and working through **both** loops of each sc, whipstitch across. Whipstitch through sts around buttonhole.
Sew Flap to side of Body Rnd 17.
Sew 1/2" (12 mm) button to side of Body opposite buttonhole.
Sew black rounded buttons to Head for eyes.
Tie ribbon in a bow around neck.

bunny

BODY, HEAD, HANDLES, & FLAP
With White, work same as Basic Purse Body, Head, Handles, and Flap, pages 2-4.

FRONT PAW (Make 2)
With White, work same as Basic Purse Paw, page 3.

BACK PAW (Make 2)
Rnds 1-10: With White, work same as Basic Purse Paw; at end of Rnd 10, do **not** finish off: 15 sc.

Rnd 11: (Sc in next 2 sc, 2 sc in next sc) around: 20 sc.

Rnd 12: (Sc in next 3 sc, 2 sc in next sc) around: 25 sc.

Rnds 13-15: Sc in each sc around.

Stuff Paw firmly between Rnds 1-12 and lightly between Rnds 13-18.

Rnd 16: (Sc in next 3 sc, decrease) around: 20 sc.

Rnds 17 and 18: Decrease around: 5 sc.

Rnd 19: (Slip st in next sc, skip next sc) twice; finish off.

Sew Back Paws to Base in a slightly horizontal position.

EAR (Make 2)
With White, ch 3; join with slip st to form a ring.

Rnd 1 (Right side)**:** Ch 1, 2 sc in each ch around; do **not** join, place marker to mark beginning of rnd: 6 sc.

Rnd 2: 2 Sc in each sc around: 12 sc

Rnd 3: (Sc in next 3 sc, 2 sc in next sc) around: 15 sc.

Rnd 4: Sc in each sc around.

Rnd 5: (Sc in next 4 sc, 2 sc in next sc) around: 18 sc.

Rnd 6: Sc in each sc around.

Rnd 7: (Sc in next 5 sc, 2 sc in next sc) around: 21 sc.

Rnd 8: Sc in each sc around.

Rnd 9: (Sc in next 6 sc, 2 sc in next sc) around: 24 sc.

Rnds 10-15: Sc in each sc around.

Rnd 16: Sc in each sc around; slip st in next sc, finish off leaving a long end for sewing.

Flatten Rnd 16, whipstitch through **both** loops of **each** stitch across.

Sew corners of Rnd 16 together, then sew Ears to top of Head with dents of Ears facing front, spacing approximately 1" (2.5 cm) apart.

CHEEK (Make 2)
With White, ch 3; join with slip st to form a ring.

Rnd 1 (Right side)**:** Ch 1, 2 sc in each ch around; do **not** join, place marker to mark beginning of rnd: 6 sc.

Rnd 2: 2 Sc in each sc around: 12 sc.

Rnd 3: (Sc in next sc, 2 sc in next sc) around: 18 sc.

Rnd 4: (Sc in next 2 sc, 2 sc in next sc) around: 24 sc.

Rnd 5: Sc in each sc around; slip st in next sc, finish off leaving a long end for sewing.

Stuff Cheeks. Sew Cheeks to lower front half of Head, with edges touching.

Instructions continued on page 20.

7

kitten

BASIC BODY, HEAD, PAWS, HANDLES, AND FLAP

With Grey, work same as Basic Purse Body, Head, Paws, Handles, and Flap, pages 2-4.

CHEEK (Make 2)

With Grey, work same as Bunny Cheek, page 6.

EAR (Make 2)
INNER EAR

Row 1 (Right side)**:** With Pink, ch 2, 2 sc in second ch from hook.

Note: Mark Row 1 as **right** side.

Rows 2-5: Ch 1, turn; 2 sc in first sc, sc in each sc across: 6 sc.

Finish off.

OUTER EAR

Rows 1-5: With Grey, work same as Inner Ear; at end of Row 5, do **not** finish off.

Joining Rnd: With **wrong** sides of Inner and Outer Ears together, working through **both** loops of sts on **both** pieces, and with Inner Ear facing; ch 1, sc evenly around entire Ear working 3 sc in each corner; join with slip st to first sc, finish off leaving a long end for sewing.

Using photo as a guide for placement, sew Ears to top of Head spaced approximately ¾" (19 mm) apart.

TAIL

Stuff Tail as you work.

With Grey, ch 3; join with slip st to form a ring.

Rnd 1 (Right side)**:** Ch 1, 2 sc in each ch around; do **not** join, place marker to mark beginning of rnd: 6 sc.

Rnd 2: (Sc in next sc, 2 sc in next sc) around: 9 sc.

Rnds 3-22: Sc in each sc around.

Rnd 23: (Sc in next 2 sc, 2 sc in next sc) around; slip st in next sc, finish off leaving a long end for sewing.

Sew Tail to Body opposite Head.

FINISHING

See Finishing, page 4.
Glue Pom-pom to Head between Cheeks for nose.

Toe Dividers: With Black, work 3 long straight stitches across end of each Paw to make Toes **(Fig. 6, page 22)**, making each stitch approximately 1" (2.5 cm) long.

9

puppy

BASIC BODY, HEAD, PAWS, HANDLES, AND FLAP
With Brown, work same as Basic Purse Body, Head, Paws, Handles, and Flap, pages 2-4.

MUZZLE
With Brown, ch 3; join with slip st to form a ring.

Rnd 1 (Right side)**:** Ch 1, 2 sc in each ch around; do **not** join, place marker to mark beginning of rnd: 6 sc.

Rnd 2: 2 Sc in each sc around: 12 sc.

Rnd 3: (Sc in next sc, 2 sc in next sc) around: 18 sc.

Rnd 4: (Sc in next 2 sc, 2 sc in next sc) around: 24 sc.

Rnd 5: (Sc in next 3 sc, 2 sc in next sc) around: 30 sc.

Rnd 6: (Sc in next 4 sc, 2 sc in next sc) around: 36 sc.

Rnds 7 and 8: Sc in each sc around.

Rnd 9: Sc in each sc around; slip st in next sc, finish off leaving long end for sewing.

Stuff Muzzle. Sew Muzzle to lower front half of Head.

NOSE
With Black, ch 3; join with slip st to form a ring.

Rnd 1 (Right side)**:** 2 Sc in each ch around; do **not** join, place marker to mark beginning of rnd: 6 sc.

Rnd 2: 2 Sc in each sc around: 12 sc.

Rnd 3: (Sc in next sc, 2 sc in next sc) around: 18 sc.

Rnd 4: Decrease around; slip st in next sc, finish off leaving a long end for sewing.

Stuff Nose. Sew Nose to Muzzle.

EAR (Make 2)
With Black, ch 3; join with slip st to form a ring.

Rnd 1 (Right side)**:** 2 Sc in each ch around; do **not** join, place marker to mark beginning of rnd: 6 sc.

Rnd 2: 2 Sc in each sc around: 12 sc.

Rnd 3: (Sc in next sc, 2 sc in next sc) around: 18 sc.

Rnds 4-7: Sc in each sc around.

Rnd 8: (Sc in next 4 sc, decrease) around: 15 sc.

Rnd 9: (Sc in next 3 sc, decrease) around: 12 sc.

Rnd 10: (Sc in next 2 sc, decrease) around: 9 sc.

Rnd 11: (Sc in next sc, decrease) around; slip st in next sc, finish off leaving a long end for sewing: 6 sc.

Flatten Rnd 11, whipstitch through **both** loops of **each** stitch across. Using photo as a guide for placement, sew Ears to sides of Head spaced approximately 3¼" (8.5 cm) apart.

Instructions continued on page 20.

11

piggy

BASIC BODY, HEAD HANDLES, AND FLAP
With Pink, work same as Basic Body, Head, Handles, and Flap, pages 2-4.

MUZZLE
With Pink, ch 7.

Rnd 1 (Right side)**:** 2 Sc in second ch from hook, sc in next 4 chs, 3 sc in last ch; working in free loops of beginning ch, sc in next 4 chs and in same st as first sc; do **not** join, place marker to mark beginning of rnd: 14 sc.

Rnd 2: 2 Sc in each of next 2 sc, sc in next 4 sc, 2 sc in each of next 3 sc, sc in next 4 sc, 2 sc in next sc: 20 sc.

Rnd 3: 2 Sc in next sc, sc in next sc, 2 sc in next sc, sc in next 5 sc, 2 sc in next sc, (sc in next sc, 2 sc in next sc) twice, sc in next 5 sc, 2 sc in next sc, sc in next sc: 26 sc.

Rnd 4: Sc in Back Loop Only of each sc around.

Rnds 5-7: Sc in both loops of each sc around.

Rnd 8: Sc in each sc around; slip st in next sc, finish off leaving a long end for sewing.

Stuff Muzzle. Sew Muzzle to lower front half of Head.

NOSTRILS
Using photo as a guide for placement and Black, work 4 long vertical straight stitches on the front of Muzzle for each Nostril **(Fig. 6, page 22)**, working Nostrils spaced approximately ¾" (19 mm) apart.

LEG (Make 4)
With Black, work same as Basic Purse Leg through Rnd 3, page 4; cut Black.

Rnds 4-11: With Pink, work same as Basic Purse Leg.

Stuff Leg.

EAR (Make 2)
Row 1: With Pink, ch 2, 2 sc in second ch from hook: 2 sc.

Row 2 (Right side)**:** Ch 1, turn; 2 sc in first sc, sc in last sc: 3 sc.

Note: Mark Row 2 as **right** side.

Rows 3-7: Ch 1, turn; 2 sc in first sc, sc in each sc across: 8 sc.

Trim: Ch 1, turn; sc around entire Ear working 3 sc in each corner; join with slip st to first sc; finish off leaving a long end for sewing.

Using photo as a guide for placement, sew Ears to Head, curving forward and spacing approximately ½" (12 mm) apart.

TAIL
With Pink; ch 8, 3 sc in second ch from hook and in each ch across; finish off leaving a long end for sewing.
Using long end, sew Tail to Body opposite Head.

FINISHING
See Finishing, page 4.

bear

BODY, HEAD, PAWS, HANDLES, AND FLAP

With Black, work same as Basic Purse Body, Head, Paws, Handles, and Flap, pages 2-4.

MUZZLE

With Brown, ch 3; join with slip st to form a ring.

Rnd 1 (Right side)**:** Ch 1, 2 sc in each ch around; do **not** join, place marker to mark beginning of rnd: 6 sc.

Rnd 2: 2 Sc in each sc around: 12 sc.

Rnd 3: (Sc in next sc, 2 sc in next sc) around: 18 sc.

Rnd 4: (Sc in next 2 sc, 2 sc in next sc) around: 24 sc.

Rnd 5: Sc in each sc around.

Rnd 6: Sc in each sc around; slip st in next sc, finish off leaving a long end for sewing.

Stuff Muzzle. Sew Muzzle to lower front half of Head.

NOSE

Using photo as a guide and Black, work several vertical straight stitches in a triangular shape approximately 1" (2.5 cm) long to form Nose on Muzzle **(Fig. 6, page 22)**; having bottom of Nose slightly above center of Muzzle. Make one vertical straight stitch down from center bottom of Nose.

EAR (Make 2)

With Black, ch 3; join with slip st to form a ring.

Rnd 1 (Right side)**:** Ch 1, 2 sc in each ch around; do **not** join, place marker to mark beginning of rnd: 6 sc.

Rnd 2: 2 Sc in each sc around: 12 sc.

Rnd 3: (Sc in next sc, 2 sc in next sc) around: 18 sc.

Rnd 4: Sc in each sc around.

Rnd 5: Sc in each sc; slip st in next sc, finish off leaving a long end for sewing.

Flatten Rnd 5, whipstitch through **both** loops of **each** stitch across.

Using photo as a guide for placement, sew Ears to sides of Head spaced aprroximately ¾" (19 mm) apart.

TAIL

With Black, ch 3; join with slip st to form a ring.

Rnd 1 (Right side)**:** Ch 1, 2 sc in each ch around; do **not** join, place marker to mark beginning of rnd: 6 sc.

Rnd 2: 2 Sc in each sc around: 12 sc.

Rnds 3 and 4: Sc in each sc around.

Rnd 5: Sc in each sc around; slip st in next sc, finish off leaving a long end for sewing.

Stuff Tail. Sew Tail to Body opposite Head.

FINISHING

See Finishing, page 4.

COW

BODY
BASE
With White, work same as Basic Purse Base, page 2.

BODY
With White, work same as Basic Purse Body through Rnd 17, page 3: 46 sc.

Rnd 18: With White sc in next 16 sc **(Fig. 4, page 22)**, with Black sc in next 3 sc, with White sc in next 4 sc, with Black sc in next 3 sc, with White sc in next 12 sc, with Black sc in next 5 sc, with White sc in next 3 sc.

Rnd 19: With White sc in next 16 sc, with Black sc in next 4 sc, with White sc in next 3 sc, with Black sc in next 6 sc, with White sc in next 9 sc, with Black sc in next 6 sc, with White sc in next 2 sc.

Rnd 20: With White sc in next 16 sc, with Black sc in next 13 sc, with White sc in next 11 sc, with Black sc in next 6 sc.

Rnd 21: With White sc in next 18 sc, with Black sc in next 11 sc, with White sc in next 11 sc, with Black sc in next 6 sc.

Rnd 22: With White sc in next 20 sc, with Black sc in next 8 sc, with White sc in next 13 sc, with Black sc in next 4 sc, with White sc in next sc.

Rnd 23: With White sc in next 22 sc, with Black sc in next 8 sc, with White sc in next 16 sc.

Rnd 24: With White sc in next 23 sc, with Black sc in next 3 sc, with White sc in next 2 sc, with Black sc in next 2 sc, with White sc in next 16 sc; cut Black.

Rnds 25-27: With White sc in each sc around.

Rnd 28: Sc in each sc around; slip st in next sc, finish off leaving a long end for sewing.

HEAD
With White, work same as Basic Purse Head, page 3.

HANDLE (Make 2)
Work same as Basic Handle, working first and last rnds in White only. For all other rnds, work 3 or 4 Black spots throughout, dropping and adding new color for desired size and shape of spot - be creative!

FLAP
With White, ch 3; join with slip st to form a ring.

Rnds 1-6: Work same as Basic Flap, page 4: 24 sc.

Rnd 7: With White sc in next 3 sc, 2 sc in next sc, with Black sc in next 3 sc, 2 sc in next sc, with White (sc in next 3 sc, 2 sc in next sc) around: 30 sc.

Rnd 8: With White sc in next 4 sc, with Black sc in next 8 sc, with White sc in next 18 sc.

Rnd 9: With White sc in next 5 sc, with Black sc in next 7 sc, with White sc in next 18 sc.

Rnd 10: With White sc in next 7 sc, with Black sc in next 5 sc, with White sc in next 18 sc.

Rnd 11: With White sc in next 7 sc, with Black sc in next 7 sc, with White sc in next 16 sc.

Instructions continued on page 18.

17

Rnd 12: With White sc in next 6 sc, with Black sc in next 4 sc, with White sc in next 2 sc, with Black sc in next 3 sc, with White sc in next 15 sc.

Rnd 13: With White sc in next 7 sc, with Black sc in next 3 sc, with White sc in next 20 sc.

Rnd 14: With White sc in next 7 sc, with Black sc in next 5 sc, with White sc in next 18 sc.

Rnd 15: With White sc in next 8 sc, with Black sc in next 4 sc, with White sc in next 18 sc.

Rnd 16: With White sc in next 10 sc, with Black sc in next 2 sc, with White sc in next 18 sc; cut Black.

Rnd 17: With White sc in each sc around; slip st in next sc, finish off leaving a long end for sewing.

MUZZLE
With Pink, ch 7.

Rnd 1 (Right side)**:** 2 Sc in second ch from hook, sc in next 4 chs, 3 sc in last ch; working in free loops of beginning ch, sc in next 4 chs and in same st as first sc; do **not** join, place marker to mark beginning of rnd: 14 sc.

Rnd 2: 2 Sc in each of next 2 sc, sc in next 4 sc, 2 sc in each of next 3 sc, sc in next 4 sc, 2 sc in next sc: 20 sc.

Rnd 3: 2 Sc in next sc, sc in next sc, 2 sc in next sc, sc in next 5 sc, 2 sc in next sc, (sc in next sc, 2 sc in next sc) twice, sc in next 5 sc, 2 sc in next sc, sc in next sc: 26 sc.

Rnd 4: 2 Sc in next sc, sc in next 2 sc, 2 sc in next sc, sc in next 6 sc, 2 sc in next sc, (sc in next 2 sc, 2 sc in next sc) twice, sc in next 6 sc, 2 sc in next sc, sc in next 2 sc; slip st in next sc, finish off: 32 sc.

Rnd 5: With **right** side facing, join White with sc in same st as slip st **(see Joining With Sc, page 22)**; sc in next 22 sc, with Black sc in next 4 sc, with White sc in next 5 sc.

Rnd 6: With White sc in next 16 sc, with Black sc in next 2 sc, with White sc in next 5 sc, with Black sc in next 4 sc, with White sc in next 5 sc.

Rnd 7: With White sc in next 3 sc, with Black sc in next 3 sc, with White sc in next 10 sc, with Black sc in next 3 sc, with White sc in next 5 sc, with Black sc in next 3 sc, with White sc in next 5 sc:; cut Black 32 sc.

Rnd 8: With White sc in each sc around; slip st in next sc, finish off leaving a long end for sewing.

Stuff Muzzle. Sew Muzzle to Head.

NOSTRILS
Using photo as a guide for placement and Black, work 6 vertical straight stitches on front of Muzzle for each Nostril **(Fig. 6, page 22)**, working Nostrils spaced approximately 1¼" (3 cm) apart.

HORN (Make 2)
Rnd 1 (Right side)**:** With Brown, ch 2, 4 sc in second ch from hook; do **not** join, place marker to mark beginning of rnd: 4 sc.

Rnd 2: Sc in each sc around.

Rnd 3: (Sc in next sc, 2 sc in next sc) twice: 6 sc.

Rnd 4: Sc in each sc around.

Rnd 5: (Sc in next sc, 2 sc in next sc) 3 times: 9 sc.

Rnd 6: Sc in each sc around.

Rnd 7: Sc in each sc around; slip st in next sc, finish off leaving a long end for sewing.

Stuff Horns. Using photo as a guide for placement, sew Horns to top of Head spaced approximately 1¾" (4.5 cm) apart.

EAR (Make 2)

Row 1 (Right side): With White, ch 2, 2 sc in second ch from hook: 2 sc.

Row 2: Sc in each sc across.

Row 3: 2 Sc in each sc across: 4 sc.

Rows 4 and 5: Sc in each sc across.

Row 6: Decrease twice: 2 sc.

Trim: Ch 1, turn; sc in each sc across; sc in end of each row across; 2 sc in free loop of beginning ch; sc in end of each row across; join with slip st to first sc; finish off leaving a long end for sewing.

Sew Ears to sides of Head below Horns.

LEG (Make 4)

With Black, ch 3; join with slip st to form a ring.

Rnd 1 (Right side): Ch 1, 2 sc in each ch around; do **not** join, place marker to mark beginning of rnd: 6 sc.

Rnd 2: 2 Sc in each sc around: 12 sc.

Rnd 3: (Sc in next 3 sc, 2 sc in next sc) around; drop Black: 15 sc.

Rnd 4: With White sc in each sc around.

Rnd 5: With White sc in next 6 sc, with Black sc in next 2 sc, with White sc in next 7 sc.

Rnd 6: With White sc in next 5 sc, with Black sc in next 5 sc, with White sc in next 5 sc.

Rnd 7: With White sc in next sc, with Black sc in next sc, with White sc in next 4 sc, with Black sc in next 4 sc, with White sc in next 5 sc.

Rnd 8: With White sc in next sc, with Black sc in next 3 sc, with White sc in next 2 sc, with Black sc in next 4 sc, with White sc in next 5 sc.

Rnd 9: With White sc in next 3 sc, with Black sc in next 5 sc, with White sc in next 7 sc.

Rnd 10: With White sc in next 4 sc, with Black sc in next 4 sc, with White sc in next 7 sc; cut Black.

Rnd 11: With White sc in each sc around; slip st in next sc, finish off leaving a long end for sewing.

Stuff Legs. Sew Legs to Base, turning each slightly to have pattern of spots vary.

TAIL

With White and leaving a long end for sewing, ch 9, slip st in back ridge of second ch from hook and each ch across **(Fig. 1, page 22)**; finish off leaving a long end for sewing.

Using long ends, sew Tail to Body.

TAIL ENDS

Cut 2 strands each of Black and White 6" (15 cm) long. Holding strands together, fold in half. Insert hook in end of Tail, draw the folded end up through Tail and pull the loose ends through the folded end; draw the knot up **tightly**. Trim ends.

FINISHING

See Finishing, page 4.

bunny
continued from page 6.

TAIL
BASE
With White, ch 3; join with slip st to form a ring.

Rnd 1 (Right side)**:** Ch 1, 2 sc in each ch around; do **not** join, place marker to mark beginning of rnd: 6 sc.

Work in Back Loops Only throughout.

Rnd 2: 2 Sc in each sc around: 12 sc.

Rnd 3: (Sc in next sc, 2 sc in next sc) around: 18 sc.

Rnd 4: (Sc in next 2 sc, 2 sc in next sc) around: 24 sc.

Rnd 5: Sc in each sc around; slip st in next sc, finish off leaving a long end for sewing.

FUR
With **right** side facing and working in free loops of sc on Rnds 1-4, join White with sc in free loop of first sc of Rnd 1 **(see Joining With Sc, page 22)**, (ch 3, sc in next sc) around; slip st in next sc; leave remaining sc on Rnd 5 unworked, finish off.

Stuff Tail. Sew Tail to Body opposite Head.

FINISHING
See Finishing, page 4.
Glue Pom-pom to Head between top of Cheeks for nose.

Toe Dividers: With Pink, work 3 long straight stitches across end of each Paw to make Toes **(Fig. 6, page 22)**, making each stitch approximately 1" (2.5 cm) long.

puppy
continued from page 10.

TAIL
Rnd 1 (Right side)**:** With Black, ch 2, 4 sc in second ch from hook: 4 sc.

Rnd 2: Sc in each sc around; do **not** join, place marker to mark beginning of rnd.

Rnd 3: (Sc in next sc, 2 sc in next sc) twice: 6 sc.

Rnds 4-6: Sc in each sc around.

Rnd 7: (Sc in next 2 sc, 2 sc in next sc) twice: 8 sc.

Rnd 8: Sc in each sc around; slip st in next sc, finish off leaving a long end for sewing.

Stuff Tail. Sew Tail to Body opposite Head.

FINISHING
See Finishing, page 4.

Toe Dividers: With Black, work 3 long straight stitches across end of each Paw to make Toes **(Fig. 6, page 22)**, making each stitch approximately 1" (2.5 cm) long.

general instructions

ABBREVIATIONS

ch(s)   chain(s)
cm   centimeters
mm   millimeters
rnd(s)   round(s)
sc   single crochet
sp(s)   space(s)
st(s)   stitch(es)
YO   yarn over

( ) or [ ] — work enclosed instructions **as many** times as specified by the number immediately following **or** contains explanatory remarks.

colon (:) — the number(s) given after a colon at the end of a row or round denote(s) the number of stitches you should have on that row or round.

GAUGE

Exact gauge is **essential** for proper size. Before beginning your Purse, make the sample swatch given in the individual instructions in the yarn and hook specified. After completing the swatch, measure it, counting your stitches and rows or rounds carefully. If your swatch is larger or smaller than specified, **make another, changing hook size to get the correct gauge**. Keep trying until you find the size hook that will give you the specified gauge.

MARKERS

Markers are used to help distinguish the beginning of each round being worked. Place a 2" (5 cm) scrap piece of yarn before the first stitch of each round, moving marker after each round is complete. Remove marker when longer needed.

CROCHET HOOKS													
U.S.	B-1	C-2	D-3	E-4	F-5	G-6	H-8	I-9	J-10	K-10½	N	P	Q
Metric - mm	2.25	2.75	3.25	3.5	3.75	4	5	5.5	6	6.5	9	10	15

Yarn Weight Symbol & Names	SUPER FINE 1	FINE 2	LIGHT 3	MEDIUM 4	BULKY 5	SUPER BULKY 6
Type of Yarns in Category	Sock, Fingering Baby	Sport, Baby	DK, Light Worsted	Worsted, Afghan, Aran	Chunky, Craft, Rug	Bulky, Roving
Crochet Gauge Ranges in Single Crochet to 4" (10 cm)	21-32 sts	16-20 sts	12-17 sts	11-14 sts	8-11 sts	5-9 sts
Advised Hook Size Range	B-1 to E-4	E-4 to 7	7 to I-9	I-9 to K-10.5	K-10.5 to M-13	M-13 and larger

CROCHET TERMINOLOGY	
UNITED STATES	**INTERNATIONAL**
slip stitch (slip st) =	single crochet (sc)
single crochet (sc) =	double crochet (dc)
half double crochet (hdc) =	half treble crochet (htr)
double crochet (dc) =	treble crochet (tr)
treble crochet (tr) =	double treble crochet (dtr)
double treble crochet (dtr) =	triple treble crochet (ttr)
triple treble crochet (tr tr) =	quadruple treble crochet (qtr)
skip =	miss

■□□□ BEGINNER	Projects for first-time crocheters using basic stitches. Minimal shaping.
■■□□ EASY	Projects using yarn with basic stitches, repetitive stitch patterns, simple color changes, and simple shaping and finishing.
■■■□ INTERMEDIATE	Projects using a variety of techniques, such as basic lace patterns or color patterns, mid-level shaping and finishing.
■■■■ EXPERIENCED	Projects with intricate stitch patterns, techniques and dimension, such as non-repeating patterns, multi-color techniques, fine threads, small hooks, detailed shaping and refined finishing.

JOINING WITH SC
When instructed to join with sc, begin with a slip knot on hook. Insert hook in stitch or space indicated, YO and pull up a loop, YO and draw through both loops on hook.

BACK RIDGE
Work only in loops indicated by arrows **(Fig. 1)**.

Fig. 1

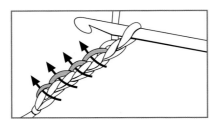

BACK LOOP ONLY
Work only in loop(s) indicated by arrow **(Fig. 2)**.

Fig. 2

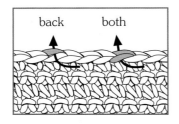

FREE LOOPS
After working in Back or Front Loops Only on a row or round, there will be a ridge of unused loops. These are called the free loops. Later, when instructed to work in the free loops of the same row or round, work in these loops **(Fig. 3a)**. When instructed to work in free loops of a chain, work in loop indicated by arrow **(Fig. 3b)**.

Fig. 3a   **Fig. 3b**

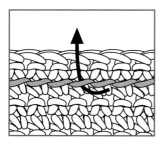 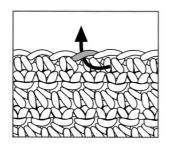

CHANGING COLORS
Insert hook in stitch indicated, YO and pull up a loop, drop yarn, with new yarn **(Fig. 4)**, YO and draw through both loops on hook. Use separate yarn for each color change.

Fig. 4

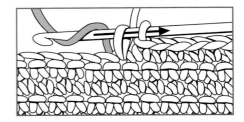

WHIPSTITCH
Sew through **both** pieces once to secure the beginning of the seam, leaving an ample yarn end to weave in later. Insert the needle from **front** to **back** through **both** loops on **both** pieces **(Fig. 5)**. Bring the needle around and insert it from **front** to **back** through next loops of both pieces. Continue in this manner across, keeping the sewing yarn fairly loose.

Fig. 5

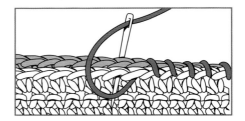

STRAIGHT STITCH
Straight Stitch is just what the name implies, a single, straight stitch. Come up at 1 and go down at 2 **(Fig. 6)**.

Fig. 6

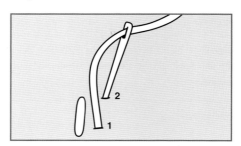

yarn information

Each Purse in this leaflet was made using Red Heart® Super Saver® Yarn. Any brand of medium weight yarn may be used. It is best to refer to the yardage/meters when determining how many balls or skeins to purchase. Remember, to arrive at the finished size, it is the GAUGE/TENSION that is important, not the brand of yarn. For your convenience, listed below are the specific colors used to create our photography models.

BUNNY
White - #311 White
Pink - #373 Petal Pink

KITTEN
Grey - #400 Grey Heather
Black - #312 Black
Pink - #373 Petal Pink

PUPPY
Brown - #336 Warm Brown
Black - #312 Black

PIGGY
Pink - #373 Petal Pink
Black - #312 Black

BEAR
Black - #312 Black
Brown - #336 Warm Brown

COW
White - #311 White
Black - #312 Black
Brown - #336 Warm Brown
Pink - #373 Petal Pink

PRODUCTION TEAM:

Instructional Editor - Lois J. Long
Contributing Technical Editor - Donna Jones
Editorial Writer - Susan McManus Johnson
Artist - Elaine Wheat
Senior Artist - Lora Puls
Photo Stylist - Sondra Daniels
Photographer - Mark Mathews

We have made every effort to ensure that these instructions are accurate and complete. We cannot, however, be responsible for human error, typographical mistakes, or variations in individual work.

©2007 by Leisure Arts, Inc., 5701 Ranch Drive, Little Rock, AR 72223. All rights reserved. This publication is protected under federal copyright laws. Reproduction or distribution of this publication or any other Leisure Arts publication, including publications which are out of print, is prohibited unless specifically authorized. This includes, but is not limited to, any form of reproduction or distribution on or through the Internet, including posting, scanning, or e-mail transmission.

ISBN-13: 978-1-60140-450-3
ISBN-10: 1-60140-450-6

Discover the *creative* world of Leisure Arts publications, where *inspiration* lives on every page.

Leaflet #3899

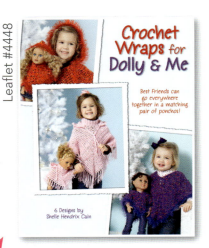

Leaflet #4448

Your next *great idea* starts here!

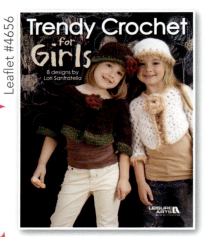

Leaflet #4656

Leaflet #3971

Leaflet #4655

Visit your favorite retailer, or shop online at leisurearts.com. For more inspiration, sign up for our free e-newsletter and receive free projects, reviews of our newest books, handy tips and more.

the art of everyday living